AMAZING ARCHITECTURE
AMAZING BRIDGES

by Anita Nahta Amin

pogo

Ideas for Parents and Teachers

Pogo Books let children practice reading informational text while introducing them to nonfiction features such as headings, labels, sidebars, maps, and diagrams, as well as a table of contents, glossary, and index.

Carefully leveled text with a strong photo match offers early fluent readers the support they need to succeed.

Before Reading

- "Walk" through the book and point out the various nonfiction features. Ask the student what purpose each feature serves.
- Look at the glossary together. Read and discuss the words.

Read the Book

- Have the child read the book independently.
- Invite him or her to list questions that arise from reading.

After Reading

- Discuss the child's questions. Talk about how he or she might find answers to those questions.
- Prompt the child to think more. Ask: Think of a bridge you have seen. Do you know what kind of bridge it is? How do you know?

Pogo Books are published by Jump!
5357 Penn Avenue South
Minneapolis, MN 55419
www.jumplibrary.com

Library of Congress Cataloging-in-Publication Data

Names: Amin, Anita Nahta, author.
Title: Amazing bridges / by Anita Nahta Amin.
Description: Minneapolis, MN: Jump!, Inc., [2023]
Series: Amazing architecture | Audience: Ages 7–10
Identifiers: LCCN 2021053851 (print)
LCCN 2021053852 (ebook)
ISBN 9781636907321 (hardcover)
ISBN 9781636907338 (paperback)
ISBN 9781636907345 (ebook)
Subjects: LCSH: Bridges
Design and construction–Juvenile literature.
Classification: LCC TG300 .A54 2023 (print)
LCC TG300 (ebook) | DDC 624.2/5–dc23/eng/20211207
LC record available at https://lccn.loc.gov/2021053851
LC ebook record available at https://lccn.loc.gov/2021053852

Editor: Eliza Leahy
Designer: Molly Ballanger

Photo Credits: Avillfoto/Shutterstock, cover; ewg3D/iStock, 1; Hien Phung Thu/Shutterstock, 3; Zastolskiy Victor/Shutterstock, 4; feblacal/iStock, 5; Imaginechina Limited/Alamy, 6-7, 16-17; Nicole Glass Photography/Shutterstock, 8; bonandbon/Shutterstock, 9; ShevchenkoAndrey/iStock, 10-11; Johnrob/iStock, 12-13; PR images/Alamy, 14; Art Wager/iStock, 15; Steve Speller/Alamy, 17; Emiralikokal/Dreamstime, 18-19; Whatiseebyme/Shutterstock, 20-21; ATGImages/iStock, 23.

Printed in the United States of America at Corporate Graphics in North Mankato, Minnesota.

TABLE OF CONTENTS

Golden Bridge,
Vietnam

CHAPTER 1

CROSSING OVER

We use bridges to get around. We walk, drive, or ride across them. A bridge is any **structure** that makes a path over an **obstacle**. Bridges can cross over roads, water, and valleys.

Civil engineers design bridges. They make blueprints. Architects help plan how bridges will look. Then, construction workers build them.

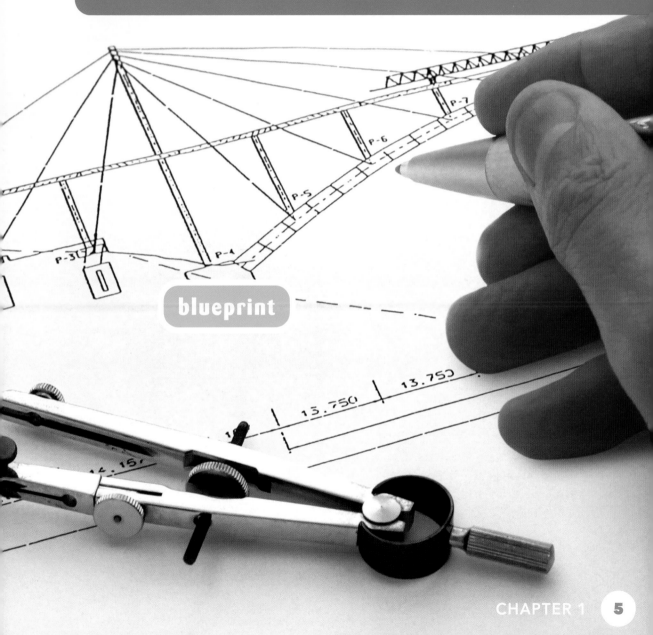

blueprint

The Danyang-Kunshan Grand Bridge in China is the longest in the world. It stretches more than 100 miles (161 kilometers)! Trains travel on it.

How do bridges like this stay up? Let's find out!

Danyang-Kunshan
Grand Bridge

CHAPTER 2

KEEP IT UP

A bridge must be strong. It needs to stand up to harsh weather. It must hold its weight and the **load** on it. Concrete and steel make strong bridges. These materials do not break under heavy loads.

The part of a bridge we walk or drive on is the deck. **Supports** hold the deck up. **Cables** are one kind of support.

cable

deck

abutment

pier

Piers are another kind. They are in the middle of a bridge. Abutments are supports on each end.

Span is the distance from one support to the next. Shorter spans give a bridge more support.

DID YOU KNOW?

Some bridges have piles. These supports are long, thin posts. They are buried deep in the ground.

Two main **forces** act on a bridge. Tension is a force that pulls. On a **suspension bridge**, the load of the deck pulls on cables. Compression is a force that squeezes or pushes. A car's weight pushes on the deck. The deck pushes on supports. This force pushes down to the ground.

suspension bridge

TAKE A LOOK!

How do forces act on a suspension bridge? Take a look!

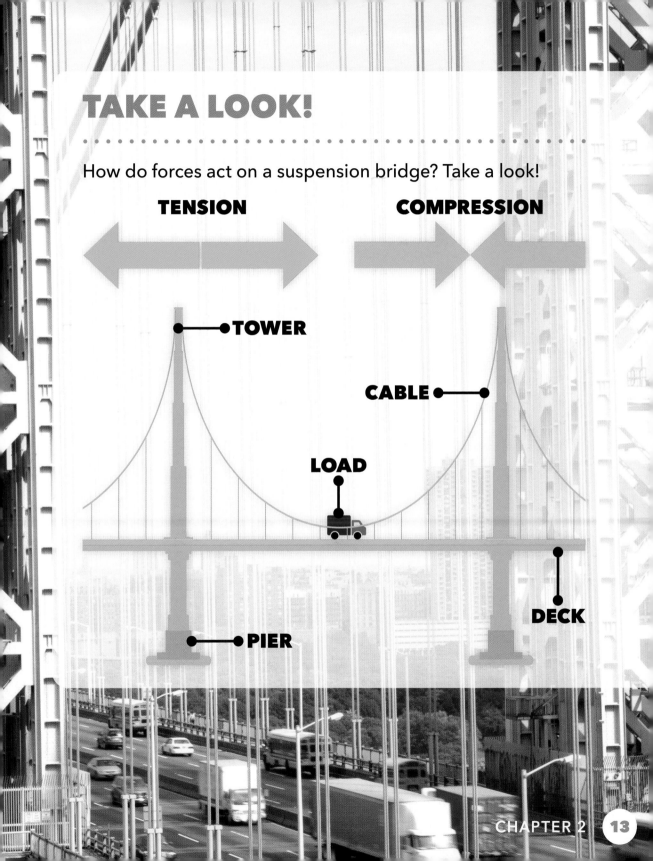

TENSION

COMPRESSION

TOWER

CABLE

LOAD

DECK

PIER

CHAPTER 3

KINDS OF BRIDGES

Some bridges cross over water. Others float on it! The SR-520 Floating Bridge in Seattle, Washington, is the longest floating bridge in the world. **Pontoons** under the deck make it float. **Anchors** hold it in place.

SR-520
Floating Bridge

The Lake Pontchartrain **Causeway** is in Louisiana. At nearly 24 miles (39 km) long, it is the longest bridge over water. More than 9,000 piles support it.

Lake Pontchartrain Causeway

Some bridges move. The Hawthorne Bridge in Portland, Oregon, lifts up. Ships pass under it. Others swing to the side. The Rolling Bridge in London, England, curls up.

Hawthorne Bridge

Rolling Bridge

Severan Bridge

The Severan Bridge in Turkey is an **arch bridge**. Arch bridges have been used for more than 3,000 years. They do not bend easily. Weight pushes on the stones under the deck. It pushes all the way down to the ground.

DID YOU KNOW?

The Severan Bridge is more than 1,800 years old. People still walk across it!

The Golden Gate Bridge in San Francisco, California, is a suspension bridge. Its two towers stand 746 feet (227 meters) above the water. Steel cables hold the deck up.

Civil engineers, architects, and construction workers work hard to make strong bridges. What kinds of bridges have you seen?

Golden Gate
Bridge

ACTIVITIES & TOOLS

TRY THIS!

TESTING BRIDGE STRENGTH

Different shapes can make a bridge stronger or weaker. See how it works with this fun activity!

What You Need:

- toothpicks
- mini marshmallows
- tape
- paper
- two paper cups
- at least 15 pennies
- notepad
- pencil or pen

1. **Put four toothpicks in a square. Stick a marshmallow on each corner to hold it together. You will need to push the toothpicks through the marshmallows so they stay. Lay the square flat.**

2. **Take four more toothpicks. Stick one into each of the marshmallows in the square so the toothpicks stand up.**

3. **Repeat Step 1 to make another square.**

4. **Attach the square from Step 3 to the structure from Step 2. You should now have a cube.**

5. **Repeat Steps 1 through 4 twice to make two more cubes. Line up the three cubes. Join them using tape. Now you have a bridge!**

6. **Place your bridge on top of two paper cups. Place a piece of paper on the bridge. This is the deck.**

7. **Place pennies on the deck one at a time until the bridge falls. Note how many pennies you placed.**

8. **Build a bridge using different shapes, such as triangles. Test how many pennies it can hold. What do you notice?**

GLOSSARY

anchors: Heavy metal objects that keep boats and other floating objects from drifting in water.

arch bridge: A bridge that mainly uses arches for support.

architects: People who design the look of structures.

blueprints: Models or detailed sketches of how structures will look.

cables: Thick ropes made of wires.

causeway: A raised road or path that crosses over wet ground or water.

civil engineers: People who design bridges, roads, and other public works.

forces: Actions that produce, stop, or change the shape or movement of objects.

load: The amount carried at one time.

obstacle: Something that is in the way.

pontoons: Shallow boats used to make a bridge float.

structure: Something that has been built.

supports: Structures that hold other things up.

suspension bridge: A bridge that is hung from cables or chains that hang from towers.

Leaderfoot Viaduct, Scotland

INDEX

TO LEARN MORE

Finding more information is as easy as 1, 2, 3.

❶ Go to www.factsurfer.com

❷ Enter "amazingbridges" into the search box.

❸ Choose your book to see a list of websites.

FACT SURFER